P9-APB-949

A New True Book

FOOTBALL

By Ray Broekel

This "true book" was prepared
under the direction of
Illa Podendorf,
formerly with the Laboratory School,
University of Chicago

CHILDRENS PRESS, CHICAGO

*The author has played football.
He has also been a Chicago Bears
fan ever since Red Grange
galloped across the gridiron.*

PHOTO CREDITS

Tony Freeman—cover, 4 (2 photos), 19, 20, 23, 25, 29

Harry and Pat Michalski—6

Ray Bruno—7

Ray De Aragon—2, 8, 21, 22, 26, 28, 30, 32, 35, 36, 37, 38, 39, 41

Michael K. Herbert—11, 12, 13, 14, 16, 43, 44

Cover—The Green Bay Packers vs. the Los Angeles Rams

Library of Congress Cataloging in Publication Data

Broekel, Ray.
   Football.

   (A New true book)
   Summary: Describes the game of football as
it is played by high school, college, and
professional teams and lists the teams and
some famous players of the National Football League.
      1.   Football—Juvenile literature.
[1.   Football]   I.   Title.
GV950.7.B75   796.332'2   81-15484
ISBN 0-516-01629-6   AACR2

New 1983 Edition
Copyright © 1982 by Regensteiner Publishing Enterprises, Inc.
All rights reserved. Published simultaneously in Canada.
Printed in the United States of America.
      5 6 7 8 9 10 R 91 90 89 88 87 86 85 84 83

TABLE OF CONTENTS

THE GAME OF FOOTBALL

It is time for the football game to start.

The two teams are lined up.

The referee blows his whistle.

The kicker boots the ball.

The game has started!

Football is played by two teams.

Each team on the field has eleven players.

Some games are played between young players.

Grade school football players

Football is played by high school teams. Many of their games are played on Friday.

College teams play most of their games on Saturday afternoons.

Jim Zorn of the Seattle Seahawks

PROFESSIONAL FOOTBALL

Professional football players get paid to play. Their games are mostly played on Sunday afternoons.

Some games are played at night.

There are 28 teams in the National Football League.

FOOTBALL UNIFORM

A football player wears a football jersey, pants, and socks.

A helmet and football shoes are worn, too.

Pads are worn under the jersey and pants. Some are shoulder pads. Some protect the hips. Other pads can be worn, too.

The uniform helps protect the player during the game.

THE PLAYING FIELD

A football field is called a gridiron. It is 100 yards long.

There are goal lines at each end of the field.

Ten yards beyond the goal lines are the goal posts. The space between the goal posts and the goal lines is the end zone.

The field has white lines every five yards. These are called yard lines.

Look at the picture. You
can see how the yards are
marked on the field. The
fifty-yard line is called
midfield.

During the game, one
half of the field belongs to
one team. The other half
of the field belongs to the
other team.

SCORING

A team can score points in four ways.

A touchdown is six points. The team must move the ball across the other team's goal line to score a touchdown.

The player who kicks the ball is on the offensive team. The quarterback sometimes holds the ball for him.

After a touchdown, the team tries to make another point. The ball must be kicked between the goal posts. This is worth one point, and is called a conversion.

Sometimes a team cannot score a touchdown. So they try for a field goal.

A field goal is three points. It is scored when the ball is kicked between the goal posts.

Sometimes a player with the ball is caught in his team's end zone. If the other team tackles him there, they score a safety. A safety is two points.

THE OFFENSIVE TEAM

The team with the ball is the offensive team.

This team tries to move the ball across the other team's goal line to score.

The offensive team must go forward ten yards in four plays, or downs. If they cannot, they must give the ball to the other team.

They give the ball to the
other team by punting, or
kicking, it to them on
fourth down.

Sometimes on fourth down the team needs only a few inches. They might keep the ball and try to make it.

If the team moves forward ten yards, they get a first down.

Then they have four more chances to move the ball ten yards.

A few inches
are sometimes
hard to get.

The offensive team
keeps moving toward the
other team's goal line.

The quarterback tells his team what to do when he calls the signals. Joe Montana, a quarterback for the San Francisco 49ers, passes the ball.

One player runs the offensive team. He is the quarterback. He can handle the ball. So can the running backs and ends.

Linemen help block the other teams' players.

The other players are called linemen. They block the other team. They try to keep the other team from getting the ball.

THE DEFENSIVE TEAM

The team without the ball is the defensive team. They try to keep the offensive team from moving the ball forward.

A defensive player can tackle the man with the ball. He can try to block a pass. He can try to catch, or intercept, a pass. He can try to get the ball if it is dropped, or fumbled.

The defensive players
have just stopped
quarterback Craig Morton
of the Denver Broncos.

Some defensive players are called linemen. They start each play facing the other team.

The players behind them are called· linebackers.

THE OFFICIALS

Sometimes a player breaks a rule. When that happens, the officials give his team a penalty. Usually his team loses yards. Sometimes they will lose a down, or play.

When a player breaks a rule, it is called a foul. The officials watch to catch any foul.

The referee is the head official.

The head linesman watches the ball move up and down the field. He keeps track of the downs.

The field judge is in
charge of timing the game.

A back judge watches
for fouls.

The officials use signals.
The signals tell what kind
of foul has been made.

THE NATIONAL FOOTBALL LEAGUE

The National Football League has 28 teams.

The teams are in two conferences.

The National Conference has three divisions.

Tony Dorsett is a famous running back for the Dallas Cowboys.

NATIONAL CONFERENCE

The Eastern Division

- Dallas Cowboys
- New York Giants
- Philadelphia Eagles
- St. Louis Cardinals
- Washington Redskins

The Central Division

- Chicago Bears
- Detroit Lions
- Green Bay Packers
- Minnesota Vikings
- Tampa Bay Buccaneers

The Western Division

- Atlanta Falcons
- Los Angeles Rams
- New Orleans Saints
- San Francisco 49ers

Jim Plunkett started as a quarterback for the San Francisco 49ers.

The American Conference also has three divisions.

AMERICAN CONFERENCE

The Eastern Division

- Baltimore Colts
- Buffalo Bills
- Miami Dolphins
- New England Patriots
- New York Jets

The Central Division

- Cincinnati Bengals
- Cleveland Browns
- Houston Oilers
- Pittsburgh Steelers

The Western Division

- Denver Broncos
- Kansas City Chiefs
- Oakland Raiders
- San Diego Chargers
- Seattle Seahawks

The Oakland Raiders and the Minnesota Vikings played in Super Bowl XI. The Raiders won 32 to 14.

THE SUPER BOWL

At the end of the season, the two best teams play each other. One team comes from the National Conference. The other team comes from the American Conference.

The two teams play in
the Super Bowl. The team
that wins is the champion
of the world.

Craig Morton
a well-known
quarterback
for the Denver Broncos

QUARTERBACKS

A quarterback is important to a football team. He runs the team, and calls the plays.

Terry Bradshaw,
a quarterback for the
Pittsburgh Steelers,
has played in
four Super Bowls.

He hands the ball off to the running backs. Sometimes the quarterback throws a pass. Sometimes he runs with the ball.

There have been many famous quarterbacks over the years.

Dan Fouts of the San Diego Chargers has just thrown a pass.

RUNNING BACKS

The running backs carry the football. They are quick. Some are fast and light. Some are big and powerful.

There have been many famous running backs.

Walter Payton, number 34, is a famous running back
who plays for the Chicago Bears.

LINEMEN

The linemen are the workhorses of a football team.

They must know how to tackle and how to block.

A defensive lineman tries to stop the other team's runners.

An offensive lineman tries to help his runners carry the ball as far as they can.

The defensive linemen of the Dallas Cowboys are in white jerseys. They will try to stop Denver from moving the ball forward. The Denver offensive linemen, in orange, will try to help their team carry the ball.

Linemen are often the
heroes of a football team.

THE FUN OF FOOTBALL

Playing football can be fun. Watching a game is fun, too.

It is great to see your favorite player score a touchdown.

And it is even better if your favorite team wins the game.

WORDS YOU SHOULD KNOW

block(BLAHK) — to keep the players on the other team from getting the ball or to the person with the ball

boot — to kick

champion(CHAM • pyun) — the winner; the best

conference(CON • fer • ence) — a group of teams

conversion (KUN • ver • zhun) — to make one point after a touchdown by kicking the football between the goal posts

defense(DEE • fence) — the team that does not have the ball

down — a football play in which a team tries to move the ball forward

end — a player on the offensive team who can handle the ball

end zone — the space between the goal posts and the goal line

famous(FAIM • us) — well known

favorite(FAIV • er • it) — liked best

field goal — three points scored by kicking the ball between the goal posts

foul — to break a rule

fumble — to drop the ball

gridiron(GRID • iron) — a football field

helmet(HEL • mit) — a head covering used to protect the head

hero — a person who does good things

intercept(in • ter • SEPT) — to catch the ball when it is passed by a player on the other team

jersey(JER • zee) — a shirt worn by football players

league(LEEG) — a group of teams that are divided into two conferences

midfield(MID • feeld) — the middle of a football field; the fifty-yard line

offense(OFF • ence) — the team that has the ball and is trying to score

official(oh • FISH • il) — the person who is in charge

pad — a cushion used to protect parts of the body

pass — to throw the ball

penalty(PEN • il • tee) — to lose yards or a down because a player breaks the rule

professional(pro • FESH • un • il) — a person paid for doing something that other people do for fun

punt — to drop the ball and kick it before it hits the ground

quarterback(KWAR • ter • back) — the player who runs the offensive team and handles the ball

referee(ref • er • EE) — the person who enforces the rules in a game

running back — a player on the offensive team who can handle the ball

safety(SAIF • tee) — tackling someone on the other team carrying the ball in his end zone. This scores two points

score(SKOR) — to get points in a game

super bowl — the football game played between the two teams who won in their conference

tackle(TACK • il) — to knock down the player carrying the ball

touchdown(TUCH • down) — to get the ball over the goal line

workhorse(WERK • horse) — a person who works very hard

INDEX

About the Author

Ray Broekel is a full-time freelance writer who lives with his wife, Peg, and a dog, Fergus, in Ipswich, Massachusetts. He has had twenty years of experience as a children's book editor and newspaper supervisor, and has taught many subjects in kindergarten through college levels. Dr. Broekel has had over 1,000 stories and articles published, and over 100 books. His first book was published in 1956 by Childrens Press.